Threads & Friends
BOOK TWO

Pedro The Pitcher's Second Chance

by Peter J. Mulry

Copyright © 2021 Peter J. Mulry. All rights reserved. Except for brief quotations for review purposes, no part of this book may be reproduced in any form without prior written permission from the author.

Published by:
Peter J Mulry Foundation

Contact the author:
peterjmulryfoundation.org
850-221-1045

Print - ISBN 978-1-7358638-2-5

I would like to thank several people who made this book possible - Lou Maggio, KR Lombardia, Gary Ippolito and Andy Taylor. I would also like to thank Mario Garcia, my Guardian Angel who has been with me through this endeavor. A tip of the cap to all the sponsors for their financial support.

Thanks to all who have helped me on my journey.

It was a bright and sunny June day when the All-Stars filed onto the field for their second game against the Tigers. The last time they played the visiting team, the All-Stars had won. Pedro the pitcher was sure they would win again. After all, the All-Stars team had won their last three games in a row. The All-Stars were unstoppable!

Coach Threads gave the team his usual pep talk, then pulled Cathy the catcher and Pedro aside. "Don't forget, since we played the Tigers before, we worked out all new signals for your pitches, Pedro. Did you two memorize them?"

Cathy nodded. "Yes, Coach."

Pedro nodded, too. But he had been extra busy playing with the new video game he got for his birthday, and hadn't spent a lot of time memorizing the signals. He figured once he was on the field, he'd be able to remember them. "Yes, Coach."

"Great. Now let's all go out there and have a great game!"

The All-Stars got into position on the field. Cathy settled behind home plate, and Pedro stepped onto the pitcher's mound. Cathy crossed two of her fingers, keeping her signal out of sight of the batter. Pedro tried to remember what that meant. Curveball? Fastball? He decided to throw a curveball.

The batter hit the ball, sending it sailing into the outfield. Before Sam could throw the ball to Freddie the first baseman, the batter had made it to first.

The next Tigers batter stepped to the plate. Cathy flicked one finger out, then made a fist. Pedro was sure that meant fastball. Yes, definitely fastball. He pitched, and the batter hit the ball hard. It sailed over Gary in the outfield, and landed in the grass. Home run.

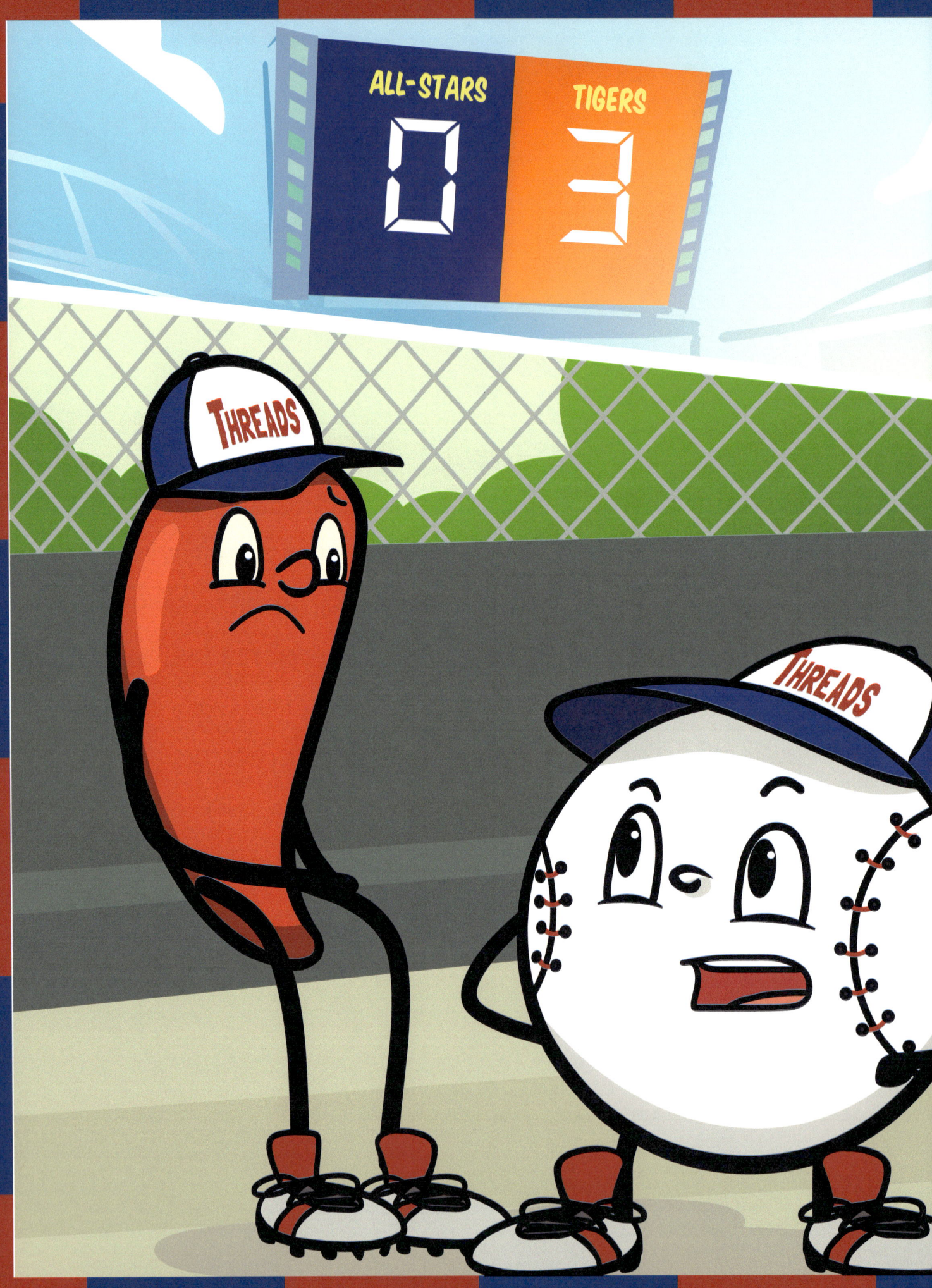

By the third inning, the Tigers were up 5 to 1. Coach Threads called Pedro into the dugout. "I asked you before the game if you memorized the new signals. And you said you did."

Pedro couldn't look Coach Threads in the eye. He studied the ground. "I don't think Cathy is doing them right."

"She's doing exactly what she's supposed to. It's not fair to blame your teammates because you aren't prepared, Pedro," Coach Threads said. "As the pitcher, you have a big responsibility to the team."

Pedro nodded. "I know."

"Responsibility means responding to the ability you have," Coach Threads said. "You have a talent, Pedro, and are a wonderful pitcher. But when you're not prepared, or not paying attention during the practices, then you're not responding to your ability. Do you know what I mean?"

Pedro raised his gaze to the coach's. "It means I should pay better attention to what you're teaching me and what the team is doing, so I can be a better pitcher."

"Exactly." Coach Threads pointed toward Cathy, sitting on the other end of the bench. "Now, why don't you do a quick run-through with Cathy of the new signals, before we get back out on the field?"

Pedro sat down beside Cathy. She handed him his water bottle and he took a sip before he spoke. "I'm sorry I didn't memorize all the new hand signals. Can we practice them now?"

"Sure." Cathy showed Pedro the signs for a curveball, a fastball, and a changeup. This time, Pedro paid attention, and by the time he knew all the signals, it was time for the All-Stars to head out to the field.

Pedro stepped onto the pitcher's mound. He was ready. When Cathy crossed two fingers, Pedro knew she meant a fastball, not a curveball. The batter swung and missed—one, two, three times. He was out!

The next Tigers' batter came up to bat. He was the same one who had hit a home run in the first inning, and Pedro was nervous. The All-Stars needed to keep the visiting team from scoring any more runs, so they could have a chance to close the gap. Pedro leaned forward a bit, to make sure he saw Cathy's signal. She flicked out one finger, then made a fist. Pedro thought for a second.

Changeup. She meant a changeup! Pedro pitched a changeup. The other batter swung and missed!

Pedro and Cathy worked together the rest of the inning, and within a few minutes, the Tigers had three outs and the All-Stars got a chance to close the gap in the score. At the end of a nail-biting game, the All-Stars won, 7-6.

"We beat the Tigers!" Cathy ran up to Pedro and gave him a high-five. "We did a great job!"

"We did," Pedro said. "Because we were a good team."

"We're the best team," Freddie the first baseman said. He had a container in his hands that his mom had given him after the game. "And speaking of being responsible, it was my turn to bring snacks. Who wants a cupcake?" The All-Stars gathered around, celebrating their victory and their friendships with cheers and cupcakes.

Threads and his Friends is a look at "Life Skills" through Baseball shared by 10 Characters representing each baseball position on the field along with the Designated Hitter. I've always believed that most "Life Skills" are easily learned with the game of baseball.

"Life Skills" such as Responsibility, Accountability, Correct Choices, Commitment, Teamwork, Hard Work, Friendship, Confidence, Honesty, and Discipline, are all part of the tools we need to give to our youth so they can grow and prosper in the game of life. As I look at our young people today, I thought these characters might be fun for them while learning "Life Skills" and some basic fundamentals at each position.

Please have fun with it!!

I would also like to thank several people who made this book possible: Lou Maggio, KR Lombardia, Gary Ippolito and Andy Taylor. Also Mario Garcia who was my Guardian Angel in this endeavor and continues to be so. A tip of the cap to all the sponsors for their financial support.

Thanks to all who have helped me on my journey.

Peter J. Mulry

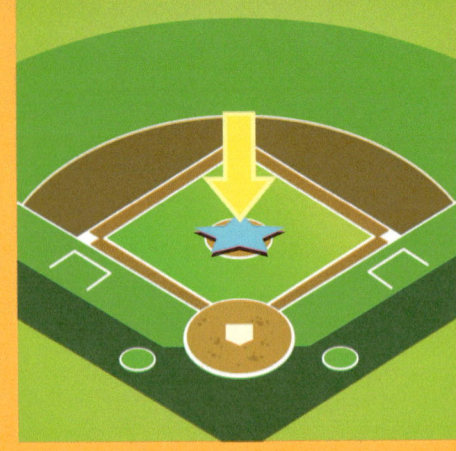

Pedro's Baseball Skills on the Field

☆ Learning how to get the right grip on a Baseball.

☆ Learning the strike zone.

☆ Learning how to get in the right position on the Pitcher's Mound.

☆ Learning wind up and proper throwing position.

☆ Learning how to pick up the Catcher's Target.

Pedro's Life Skills on the Field

Responsibility

- Willingness - Pay attention to coaches.
- Acceptance - Be a good teammate.
- Responsive - Pay attention to all situations in a game and be alert.
- Talent - Do your best and try your hardest.

Cathy
the Catcher

Cathy's Baseball Skills on the Field

☆ Learning how to put on the catcher's equipment.

☆ Learning the strike zone and where the target should go.

☆ Learning how to grip the ball.

☆ Telling teammates game situations and making her teammates aware of them.

Cathy's Life Skills on the Field

Accountability

- **Willingness** - To learn the rules of how to play the game.
- **Accountability** - Keeping herself and her teammates on the right track by being a leader.
- **Decision Making** - Making the right choices.
- **Measurement** - Knowing the rules. Knowing the count (balls, strikes, outs)

Freddie
the 1st Baseman

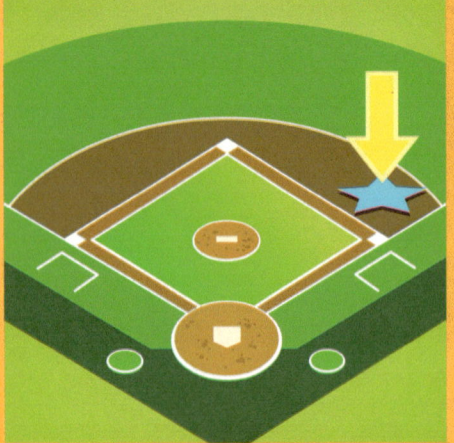

Freddie's Baseball Skills on the Field

☆ Knowing when a ground ball is hit to go to first base and put your heels on each corner of the base and be able to reach out for the ball.

☆ Learn how to use a first baseman's mitt. It will help make plays a regular glove can't—example a ball in the dirt coming from another infielder.

☆ Learning how to be the cut-off man for the balls hit to the outfield.

☆ Responsible for bunts on the right side of the field-when the situation calls for it.

Freddie's Life Skills on the Field

Correct Choices

Perception - Freddie learns by knowing what's going on every pitch during the game and what needs to be done.

Comprehension - Understand the game situation and pay attention.

Action - Taking the steps and making the choices to do what needs to be done on each play and doing it.

Manners - Know that there is a "Baseball Etiquette" when playing. "The Do's and Don'ts of the Game"

Sam
the 2nd Baseman

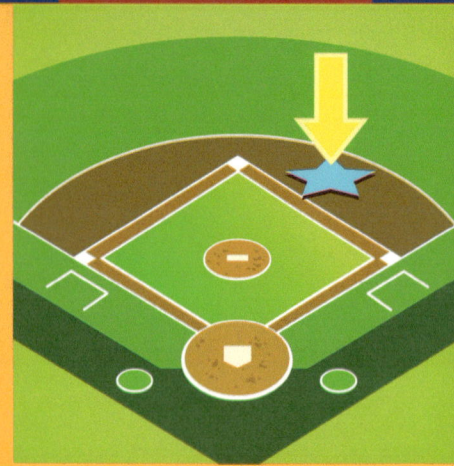

Sam's Baseball Skills on the Field

☆ Ground Balls hit to the 2nd baseman will go to first base.

☆ Ground balls hit to the shortstop or 3rd baseman with runners on 1st base-the 2nd baseman needs to go to second to get the throw for a force-out.

☆ In bunt plays he needs to cover first base-for the first baseman may need to field a bunt.

☆ Balls hit to the right side of the outfield—he will need to be the relay man.

Sam's Life Skills on the Field

Commitment

Conduct - Plays in a spirit of good sportsmanship.

Consistent - Belief of always giving his best on the field to himself and his team.

Sacrifice - Learning to take a little less to help one of his teammates.

Hustle - Never walk on and off the field without giving positive energy.

Samantha
the Shortstop

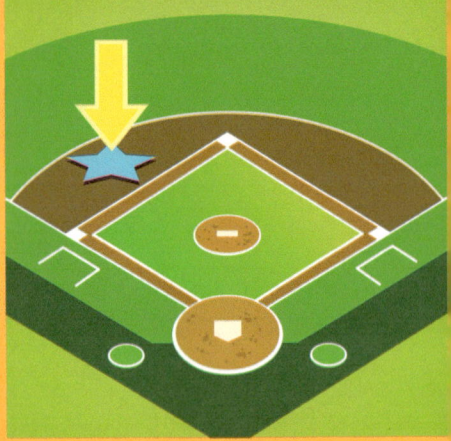

Samantha's Baseball Skills on the Field

☆ Needs the strongest throwing arm because she will make the longest throws in the infield.

☆ With a runner on first or second base and a round ball is hit to the right side she needs to cover 2nd base for a force out.

☆ In all bunt situations she needs to cover 2nd base for a possible force play.

☆ The shortstop is the relay person to the outfield from anywhere on the left side of the field.

Samantha's Life Skills on the Field

Attitude

Cooperation - She blends in with the team to get everyone to do their part. "She's a leader."

Common Goal - The common goal is to be the best we can with individuals working together to win as a team.

Respect - She knows that everyone has their own job to do and gives them encouragement to do that.

Selfless - Putting the team first-there is no "I" in team.

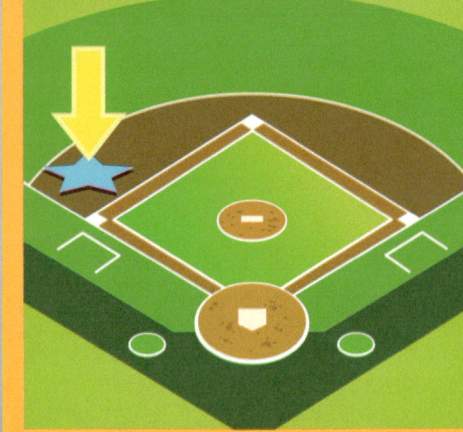

Gary
the 3rd Baseman

Gary's Baseball Skills on the Field

☆ The third baseman needs to have quick reactions because ground balls get to him the quickest.

☆ He needs to cover the left side on bunt plays.

☆ With a runner on first base he needs to throw to second base on ground balls for a force out.

☆ He is the relay man for balls hit into left with a runner on second base.

Gary's Life Skills on the Field

Hard Work

Discipline - Working hard every day on the field to become the best he can be. "Pay attention to the game."

Results - The end of game is determined by what you have done during the game.

Courage - Learn not to be afraid of the ball.

"Done is Never" - If you're going to be great at anything in your life you never stop working and getting better—catching ground balls every day.

Louie
the Left Fielder

Louie's Baseball Skills on the Field

☆ Learning to catch fly balls. The best way to do this is start by using a softer ball than regular baseball.

☆ Must learn how to throw the ball a longer distance for he will make strong throws back to the infield.

☆ Needs to be taught how to long toss.

☆ His basic territory is from his position to the leftfield line.

☆ Must learn with runners on base when the ball is hit to him which base he should throw to.

Louie's Life Skills on the Field

Friendship

Trust - Trusts his coaches and teammates to do the right things and make the right decisions so his team does well.

Honesty - Being truthful to his coaches and teammates. "Louie's always honest."

Connection - Getting close to his teammates who are part of a common goal. "Lifetime contacts"

Compassion - When teammates make a mistake or a wrong play he helps them with encouraging remarks.

Chen
the Center Fielder

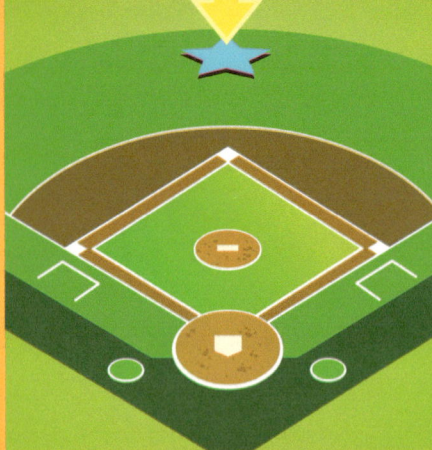

Chen's Baseball Skills on the Field

☆ Since he has the best view of the hitter he needs to get a good jump on the ball and be ready to back up his fellow outfielders.

☆ Runs to a spot where he feels the ball will be—"anticipate"

☆ Catches fly balls with his glove up. Good rule to learn is if ball is below the belly button the glove is down. If ball is above the belly button the glove is up.

☆ Knows every situation when runners are on base so he knows where the ball should go.

Chen's Life Skills on the Field

Confidence

Purpose - Always a reason for every play made on a baseball field.

Expecting - Chen wants every ball hit to him—he knows his position and everyone else on the field and knows what to do!

Tenacious - He lets everyone know in the outfield what the situation is before each pitch—he is the leader in the outfield.

Study - Always wanting to learn and get better.

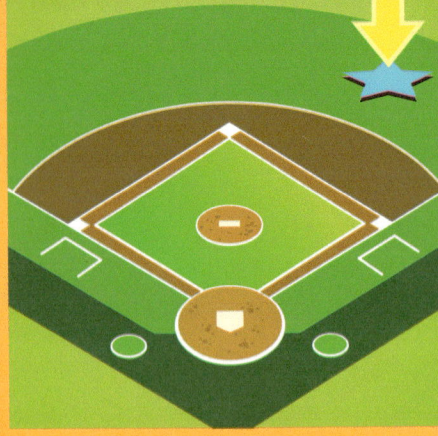

Rita
the Right Fielder

Rita's Baseball Skills on the Field

☆ Don't be afraid to go to one knee when a ground ball is hit to you.

☆ Be ready to cover all the way to the right field line.

☆ Back up balls hit to the centerfielder and the first baseman.

☆ Always be ready with runners on base if the ball is hit to us—which base are we throwing to—the right fielder is usually the outfielder who has the best arm.

Rita's Life Skills on the Field

Honesty

Truth - Being honest with herself and the situations around her.

Integrity - Don't cheat to win.

Sincere - Being honest.

Be true to yourself in the game, if it doesn't feel right tell your coaches.

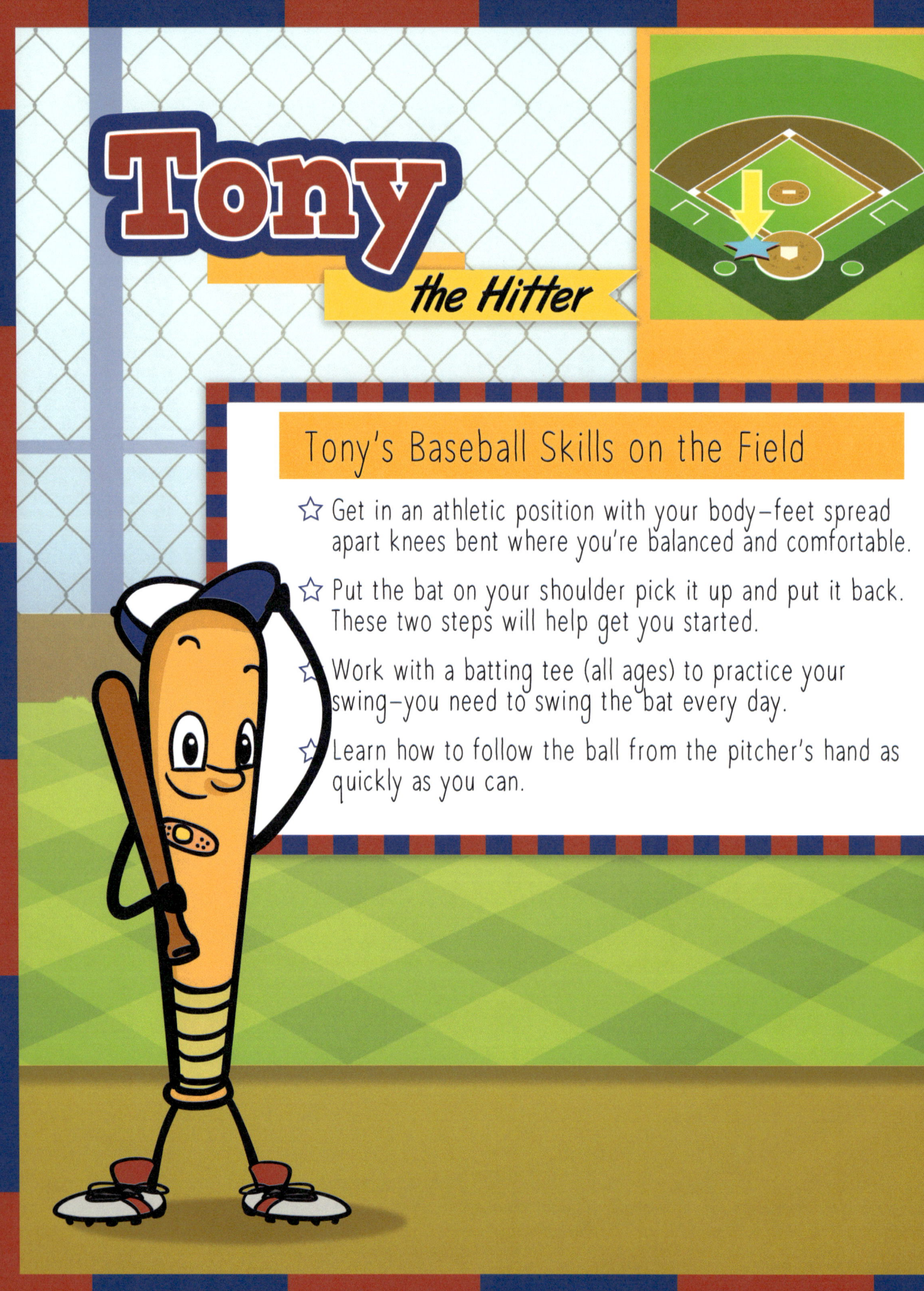

Tony the Hitter

Tony's Baseball Skills on the Field

☆ Get in an athletic position with your body—feet spread apart knees bent where you're balanced and comfortable.

☆ Put the bat on your shoulder pick it up and put it back. These two steps will help get you started.

☆ Work with a batting tee (all ages) to practice your swing—you need to swing the bat every day.

☆ Learn how to follow the ball from the pitcher's hand as quickly as you can.

Tony's Life Skills on the Field

Discipline

Instruction - Learning to listen to coaches and instructors how to hit and get into the right hitting position.

Repetition - Learning that to be good at anything you have to do it again and again the correct way.
"Perfect practice makes perfect."

Self Control - Knowing that anything worth doing takes time and you have to have patience with yourself.
"Don't get mad."

Practice - Is the only way to get better at anything we do. However doing the right things at practice is the key.

Coach's Corner
FINANCIAL AWARENESS

Goal Setting

In this story, Pedro is a good pitcher who was not responsible when he was supposed to learn the different pitching signs. Coach Threads reminded him that responsibility means responding to your ability. Pedro realized that he needed to work with Cathy to learn the signs so that he could help his team. Setting goals to be a better player or student is important for your future.

What is your goal for the future?

Short-term goals are goals that you want to achieve soon, such as in two weeks or a few months.

What is your short-term goal?

About the Author

Pete Mulry, one of the winningest coaches in high school baseball, coached for ten years at Tampa Catholic High School, and left that job with an overall high school record of 329-39. His team won State Championships in '68, '71, '73, and '76 and a National Championship in '73. He was honored as Florida Coach of the year in 1968, 1971, 1973 and  1976 and Nominated for National Coach of the year in 1977. Pete then moved on to the collegiate level, coaching the University of Tampa from 1978 through 1982. He also scouted for KC. Royals. He was recently honored by the Tampa Tribune as one of the Top 50 coaches in athletics in the Tampa Bay area. He has dedicated his life, and his foundation, the Peter J. Mulry Foundation, to teach young children life skills through sports.

Look for the next book in this fun series!

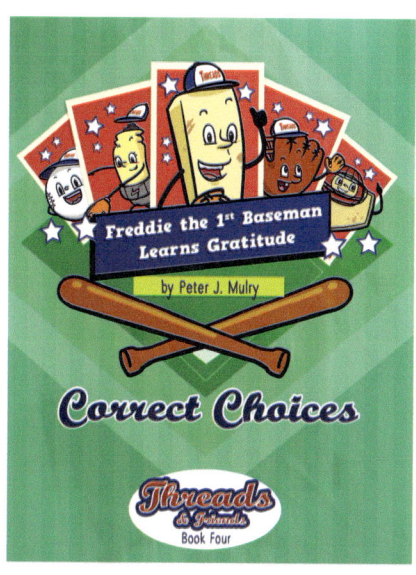

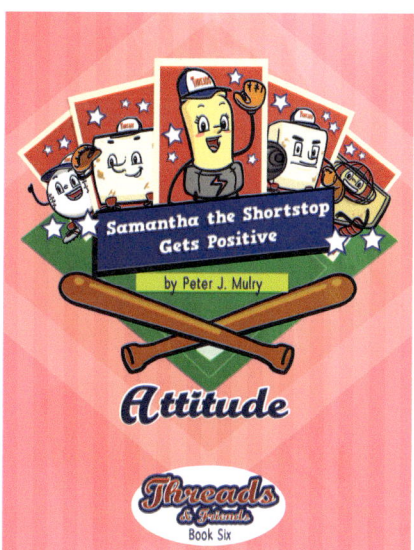

Made in the USA
Columbia, SC
20 July 2024

39046626R00031